Summary

of

Master Slave
Husband Wife:

An Epic Journey from Slavery to
Freedom

Chris Franklin

Table of Contents

CHAPTER I

Intro

The incredible true story of Ellen Craft, who, with William acting as "his" slave and Ellen passing for a wealthy, crippled White man, escaped enslavement via audacity, perseverance, and disguise.

A young, enslaved couple named Ellen and William Craft accomplished one of the most daring acts of self-emancipation in American history in 1848, a year of global democratic uprising. They rode in the open on steamboats, carriages, and trains as they travelled from Georgia's bondage to the free states of the North while assuming the roles of master and slave and being sustained by their love as husband and wife.

They avoided being discovered along the way by slave dealers, military personnel, and even friends of their captors. The story of their expedition quickly made them famous and made national news. The captivating young couple, who toured another 1,000 miles across New England while receiving tremendous ovation as they talked alongside some of the biggest abolitionist figures of the day, including Frederick Douglass and William Wells Brown, were in high demand among Americans.

Even so, they were still in danger. After the horrific New Fugitive Slave Act was passed in 1850, all Americans were responsible for sending back fugitives like the Crafts to slavery. Slave hunters arrived from Georgia, forcing the Crafts to flee once more, this time from the United States, where the stakes were higher than ever. This was the start of yet another adventure.

Master Slave Husband Wife is an American love story that would question the country's fundamental principles of life, liberty, and justice for all. It still confronts us now since it condenses three epic journeys into one massive attempt for liberation.

CHAPTER II

In a top hat and cravat, escaping slavery

In Macon, Georgia, a few days before Christmas in 1848, Ellen Craft, a slave, wore a stovepipe hat. The hat completed Craft's risky disguise, which she used to travel all the way to Pennsylvania in a series of trains, steamboats, and carriages while appearing to be a white man. Ellen disclosed to other tourists that she was a planter travelling to the north for medical attention. William, her enslaved husband, accompanied her while posing as her property.

The ploy succeeded. But that was not where their story ended. The Crafts were well-known abroad when the American Civil War started. The marriage also had a significant impact on the series of events that resulted in the Civil War and the abolition of slavery, as Ilyon Woo demonstrates in her superb new book, "Master Slave Husband Wife."

It all began with a scheme that some sources, including Woo, attribute to Ellen. Ellen was born a slave to her own father, James Smith, a white plantation owner who also sold Maria, Ellen's mother, who was then 18 years old, into slavery. Maria was not protected from rape by her master under the laws of slavery, and in 1837, probably because to Ellen's fair complexion and physical similarity to Smith, Smith's wife gave Ellen to their daughter Eliza as a wedding present when she wed Macon's Robert Collins.

Ellen met and fell in love with William Craft in Macon, Georgia, while he was an enslaved cabinetmaker who was legally owned by her half sister. They both had unpleasant experiences being separated from family members. The move of Ellen from Smith's plantation to Collins's home tore her from her mother. When their beloved sister was sold at a public auction when they were children, William was irrevocably taken away from her. The Crafts made the decision to carry out their escape plan as 1848 came to an end because they were determined not to be separated from one another or to have children who might be sold away from them.

With flashbacks to their earlier lives intermingled, the first half of "Master Slave Husband Wife" is a thrilling, delicately handled narrative of their four-day trek to the North. Woo, who previously wrote "The Great Divorce," a book about a scandal involving a fighting marriage and the Shaker religious sect in the 1810s, reveals how they were able to pull it off along the road. Ellen's outfit, which comprised dark green glasses, a sling for her right arm, a black cravat, and that "double-story" silk hat, "befitting how high it climbs, and the narrative it covers," was an important component of the strategy. Ellen also wore bandages on her face and hand to give the impression that she was the ill young scion of a wealthy family, travelling across the Mason-Dixon line with a devoted manservant to consult with a doctor. They boarded train cars and entered dining halls full of white travellers. She was able to conceal the fact that she had never been permitted to learn how to write her name by using her wounded hand as an easy excuse for why she was unable to sign travel documents at a number of destinations.

Woo uses a cinematic approach to tell the tale of that disguise and the adventure it started. She is an expert scene-setter, bringing to life the emotions felt by the Crafts at each terrifying moment: the sound of "Ellen's boot heels clacking down hard with every step up the gangway" to a steamboat in Savannah; the soothing scent of the poultice William delicately applied to her face before she went to sleep in her berth, "freshly plastered in reeking flannel."

Woo is able to communicate the Crafts' attention to detail by using the evocative details in their story.. It's safe to say that Ellen's ability as a seamstress helped her modify the clothing she wore. William had saved money by doing carpentry work for clients who were willing to pay an enslaved man a pittance. He had used that money to buy parts of her costume.

The fugitives, however, valued Ellen's hard-earned understanding of young white men's habits even more because she acquired it while working in the Collinses' private quarters. William also knew how to play the part that white Southerners on the trip expected him to play: that of an obedient servant eager to anticipate his ill master's every need.

Above all, their deception was successful due of the privileges enjoyed by white male

Southerners at first glance. Ellen Craft, according to Woo, "now had boundless mobility across the streets she had previously been forbidden to roam without a pass," as a white man's son. The compelling argument made in "Master Slave Husband Wife" is that the Crafts' escape exposed and subverted the shaky roots of the gendered and raced identities of master and slave.

However, even in the North, the pair remained in danger. Woo's story briefly slows down to educate readers on the politics surrounding the enactment of the Fugitive Slave Law of 1850 after following the Crafts from Philadelphia to Boston, where they landed after spending some time on the antislavery lecture circuit.

The narrative takes up again as she describes the widespread opposition to the infamous law among Black Bostonians and their white friends. When Robert Collins despatched two agents to Boston to arrest the Crafts, the law's enforcement would undergo its first real test.

The couple was determined to oppose re-enslavement by whatever means necessary in the confrontations that took place in Boston's courts and streets; William repeatedly flashed a pistol and made it known he would use it. Collins' operatives were ultimately unsuccessful, hindered in part by uncertainty among authorities on the recently passed Fugitive Slave Law. Nevertheless, it was obvious that the slave catchers would return.

The Crafts left the United States because they felt unsafe there, and they eventually made their way to England. There, in 1860, they published a story about their escape called "Running a Thousand Miles for Freedom," which helped the transatlantic pressure campaigns that sped up the sectional crisis over slavery. Along with fellow fugitive and abolitionist William

Wells Brown, William travelled the world giving lectures.

While navigating the contentious politics of the British antislavery movement, Ellen started parenting their six children. And the formal education that had been denied to them while they were slaves was pursued by the husband and wife.

Although Ellen could not totally escape the social order that she had distorted to her advantage while posing as a white man, Woo claims that their partnership continued to defy convention even while they were living in England. Despite her objections, abolitionists frequently referred to her as a "white slave," including her husband, and William Craft alone was given credit for writing their book.

Even though Ellen played the main part and may have come up with the escape plot, according to Woo, he simply referred to her as "my wife" throughout the story and stated that she at first opposed it.

Although Ellen, who had formerly impersonated a master, "assumed narrative control," too, at certain crucial moments, there are less traces of her voice in the archival record than there are of William's, according to Woo. One outstanding accomplishment of Woo's book is its attentive focus on the rare occasions when Ellen Craft's perspective does emerge from the archive, such as in a signed letter, an overheard song, or an acerbic laugh directed at a minister, as well as its in-depth analysis of what her silences might mean.

In a quick but poignant finale, Woo also considers a final blank in the records: the precise day and reason for Ellen Crafts' passing after the Crafts, remarkably, had returned to the American South after the Civil War. After a perilous and depressing 20 years in the post-Reconstruction South, with twists and turns that could fill many more pages, Ellen would be laid to rest under a tree in Georgia.

However, Woo rightfully deserves to devote her entire book to the portion of her tale that she chooses to convey. Wendell Phillips, a well-known abolitionist, made the following prediction shortly after the Crafts managed to escape: "Future historians and poets would relate this narrative as one of the most stirring in the nation's annals, and millions would read it with admiration for the hero and heroine." He was correct, and Woo's work ought to add to those throngs of fans, particularly of her heroine.

CHAPTER III

A compelling story that effectively conveys the tenacity and bravery of a magnificent pair.

An interesting story about the struggle for freedom of one slave couple and the power of their unbreakable love.

What are the characteristics of enduring love and dedication, and how may devoted lovers overcome their challenges? The Great Divorce author Woo provides readers with the answers to these concerns by taking them on an exciting journey with Ellen Craft (1826-1891) and William Craft (1824-

1900), who put their lives in danger in order to flee slavery in Georgia in 1848.

The content "is not fabricated," which is refreshing. Starting with the Crafts' own 1860 story, Running a Thousand Miles for Freedom, every description and piece of dialogue comes from historical sources. The Crafts escaped as national discussions over slavery raged, starting a difficult path to assert their right to emancipation. No Underground Railroad helped them leave the South, the author claims. "They moved like clockwork using the most advanced transportation methods available at the time, including steamboats, stagecoaches, and—most importantly—an actual railroad—riding the tracks built by the enslaved. Empowered by their pretence as master and slave, by the actuality of their love as husband and wife. William played the part of Johnson's devoted slave, while Ellen, who "could pass for White," assumed the identity of the affluent "disabled" Mr. Johnson.

They avoided curious spectators and determined slave catchers operating under the auspices of the Fugitive Slave Act as they travelled from Macon, Georgia, up through Philadelphia, Boston, and Halifax. The Crafts also started attending abolitionist conferences. They ran the risk of being discovered and sent back to their owners—one of whom was Ellen's half-sister—after speaking to crowded audiences. The Crafts gained faith in local abolitionists as a result of their protection and celebration by them. They consented to live public lives, finally made their way to England, where they settled down, began families, and kept telling their story. Woo writes gripping stories that are masterfully told.

An engrossing story that effectively conveys the tenacity and bravery of an extraordinary couple.

CHAPTER IV

The Cottage(An Excerpt)

In the early morning hours of Macon, Georgia, there is no movement in the city. The tall, dark pines are barely stirred by the cold, windless air. Cotton Avenue is also silent, with the enormous weighing scales temporarily hidden behind shut warehouse doors. A slave couple, however, moves in a cabin in the shadow of a large, white mansion while the Ocmulgee River rushes down the eastern coast, ready to transform.

These last few nights, while they practised the motions they presently do, they hardly got any sleep. Although Ellen needs to alter her figure in various ways, such as flattening or binding the swell of her breasts, she removes her gown and forgoes a corset for once. She dons a white blouse, a long vest, a baggy coat, skinny jeans, and a lovely cloak to cover it all up. She fastens the buttons and takes a breath in the chilly December air. Christmas will soon be here.

She gets ready by candlelight, which flickers throughout the cottage, "her" workshop, which is secured with the least valuable key in case she is discovered. Her working instruments are all about her—workbaskets filled with pins, scissors, linen, needles, and thread. Additionally, wood furniture made by her husband, including a chest of drawers that is now unlocked, is visible.

Ellen puts on a pair of sturdy, thick-soled gentleman's boots. Despite her practise, they must feel unusual because each sole is being pulled an additional inch to the ground by an inch of leaden weight. The light skin of her father may have been passed down to Ellen, but not his height. She's tiny, even for a lady.

William towering over her and movements while creating a long shadow. They need to gather and pack her freshly cut hair so they can do something with it. If you leave it behind, you're giving the person who eventually bursts through the door a hint.

The finishing touches include a silky black cravat and bandages. One is wrapped over Ellen's chin, while the other is around the hand she is holding in a sling. She has extra-tall silk hat that William refers to as a "double-story" hat because of how high it climbs and the fiction it covers, green-tinted glasses, and greater protection for her face. These embellishments cover off her scars, her fear, and her smoothness.

The altered Ellen is now positioned in the middle of the floor. She appears to be a young, White, sickly man—"a highly respectable-looking gentleman," as her spouse described her. He is prepared as well, wearing his typical shirt and slacks with just one new addition—a white, used beaver hat that is nicer than anything he has ever worn and signifies the status of a wealthy man's slave.

To think that it had only been a few days. Four days had passed since they originally endorsed the notion and declared it feasible. Clothing packing, purchasing, route planning, and sewing took up four days. They would assert that they had four days to get ready for the marathon of a lifetime. Or, a lifetime of training focused on this.

CHAPTER V

About the Author

Ilyon Woo

Ilyon Woo, who has won a Whiting Creative Nonfiction Writing Grant, is the author of The Great Divorce: A Nineteenth-Century Mother's Extraordinary Fight Against Her Husband, the Shakers, and Her Times. She has received funding for her study from the National Endowment for the Humanities among other organisations, and her pieces have featured in publications including The Boston Globe and The Wall Street Journal. She graduated from Yale College with a BA in Humanities and Columbia University with a PhD in English.

Made in the USA
Las Vegas, NV
04 September 2023

77056124R10015